A Warm Heart
AND OTHER STORIES

A Warm Heart

AND OTHER STORIES

Twenty-five anecdotes from the life of

HARAV AHARON YEHUDAH LEIB SHTEINMAN ZT"L

accompanied by authentic, touching illustrations that bring
each story to life

RABBI AVRAHAM OHAYUN
ILLUSTRATED BY TAMAR ZEITLIN

Copyright © 2016 by Israel Bookshop Publications
Second Printing 2018

ISBN 978-1-60091-471-3

Translated by M. Gendelman

Published by:
Israel Bookshop Publications
501 Prospect Street
Lakewood, NJ 08701

Tel: (732) 901-3009
Fax: (732) 901-4012
www.israelbookshoppublications.com
info@israelbookshoppublications.com

Printed in Ukraine

Distributed in Israel by:
Shanky's
Petach Tikva 16
Jerusalem
972-2-538-6936

Distributed in Europe by:
Lehmanns
Unit E Viking Industrial Park
Rolling Mill Road,
Jarrow, Tyne & Wear NE32 3DP
44-191-430-0333

Distributed in Australia by:
Gold's Book and Gift Company
3-13 William Street
Balaclava 3183
613-9527-8775

Distributed in South Africa by:
Kollel Bookshop
Northfield Centre
17 Northfield Avenue
Glenhazel 2192
27-11-440-6679

Table of Contents

BIOGRAPHICAL SKETCH OF MARAN HARAV AHARON YEHUDAH LEIB SHTEINMAN ZT"L

A Warm Heart is a book of twenty-five true, inspirational stories about Maran Harav Aharon Yehudah Leib Shteinman *zt"l*.

Rav Aharon Leib was born in Europe, in the city of Brisk, in Cheshvan of 5674. His father, Reb Noach Tzvi Shteiman (Rav Aharon Leib's original last name) was the *shamash* of a shul, and he was also in charge of the *eiruv* in the city.

Rav Aharon Leib learned in *cheder* for the first few years of his childhood, but already at age eleven he went on to learn in Yeshivas Toras Chessed in Brisk. He became very close to the *rosh yeshivah*, Harav Moshe Sokolovsky, even *davening* with him in the *minyan* in his home, and he also gained much from the *mashgiach* of the yeshivah, Harav Avraham Yaakov Gordon.

At the age of sixteen, Rav Aharon Leib traveled to the city of Kobrin, to learn under Harav Pesach Pruskin. For about six months Rav Aharon Leib sat and learned there, until the yeshivah in Kobrin closed down due to lack of funding. After that he returned to Yeshivas Toras Chessed.

Rav Aharon Leib enjoyed a close relationship with the *rabbanim* of the city of Brisk, including Harav Simchah Zelig Riger (a cousin of his mother), who gave him *semichah*, and the Brisker Rav, Harav Yitzchak Zev Soloveitchik.

While Rav Aharon Leib wanted nothing more than to simply sit and learn in peace, in was not meant to be. He soon received a draft from the Polish army, something that everyone—and especially a *ben Torah*—tried to avoid at all costs. Rav Aharon Leib changed his last name from "Shteiman" to "Shteinman," hoping that this would make the Polish army think he was an only child (after all, there were no other "Shteinmans" who could be his siblings), and they would therefore leave him alone.

Unfortunately, his plan did not work; the army persisted in their demands of him. Seeing this, Rav Shteinman decided to escape to Switzerland. Two grandsons of Harav Chaim Soloveitchik (Rav Chaim Brisker), Rav Moshe Soloveitchik and Rav Aryeh Leib Glikson, went along with him.

In Montreux, Switzerland, Rav Aharon Leib soon became *rosh mesivta* of the yeshivah Eitz Chaim, which was led by Harav Eliyahu Botschko. But even there Rav Aharon Leib did not have peace and quiet. World War II broke out, and Rav Aharon Leib was taken, along with other foreign citizens, to a forced labor camp.

Through a miracle, Rav Aharon Leib succeeded in evading the terrible, backbreaking work in the camp: Someone told a tuberculosis patient to spit into Rav Aharon Leib's tuberculosis test, thereby causing Rav Aharon Leib's test to come out positive. The authorities then granted him, the new "tuberculosis patient," a reprieve from the forced labor.

In Teves of 5704, Rav Aharon Leib married Rebbetzin Tamar, the daughter of Rav Shammai

Shraga Kornfeld. There were very few guests in attendance at the wedding, as Rav Aharon Leib was very firm about keeping the *chasunah* costs to a minimum, since it was being paid for by the *tzedakah* money of others. A year later, Rav Shteinman and his wife decided to move to Eretz Yisrael, where they settled in the city of Bnei Brak.

At first, Rav Shteinman learned in a *beis midrash* in Petach Tikvah, where his *chavrusa* was Harav Chaim Shaul Karelitz. Then, about six months later, at the recommendation of the Chazon Ish, Rav Shteinman became *rosh yeshivah* of Yeshivas Chafetz Chaim in Kfar Saba.

A few years later, Rav Yosef Shlomo Kahaneman, the Ponovezher Rav, set his eye on the outstanding young *talmid chacham* and appointed him as *rosh yeshivah* of the Ponovezher Yeshivah L'tze'irim. Sometime after that, Rav Kahaneman asked Rav Aharon Leib to be the *rosh kollel* of the Ponovezher Kollel, as well.

From then on, Rav Shteinman acted as *rosh yeshivah* for many different *yeshivos*: Yeshivah Gaon Yaakov, where he gave an afternoon *shiur*; Yeshivah Orchos HaTorah, which he himself established; Yeshivah Rinah Shel Torah; Ner Zorei'ach; and Torah B'tifartah.

At the urging of Harav Shach, Rav Aharon Leib joined the Moetzes Gedolei HaTorah of the Degel HaTorah party, and after Rav Shach's *petirah*, he became known as the leader of the *Litvishe frum* community, together with Harav Elyashiv.

Rav Shteinman authored many *sefarim* on Shas, Chumash, and the Haggadah, under the title *Ayeles Hashachar*. He also wrote other *sefarim* on topics of *mussar* and on the Yamim Tovim.

Rav Shteinman's holy lifestyle, the way he tried to avoid all *gashmiyus*, and his deep care and concern for all that would affect the *frum* community, are awe-inspiring. He guided and advised many important organizations, such as Kupat Ha'ir, Lev L'achim, and Chinuch Atzmai. Those who were privileged to see this *gadol*, to hear him speak, and to receive his blessing, felt that they were standing in the presence of a giant—a ladder whose feet were planted on the ground but whose head reached up to the sky.

On 24 Kislev 5778, the bitter news struck the Torah world: Rav Shteinman was *niftar*. He was 104 years old. His *levayah* was attended by thousands, although, in his great humility, he specifically requested that no *hespedim*, praise, or honorary titles be given for him.

This book attempts to give you a tiny glimpse into the greatness of Rav Shteinman. It provides a small window into the world of his pure Torah learning, his holiness, and his special ways.

BY THESE LINES I LIVE MY WHOLE LIFE!

One day, Rav Yitzchak Zilberstein entered Rav Shteinman's room, accompanied by a young man.

"We have a question regarding a *bachur* who is in desperate need of a *yeshuah*," Rav Zilberstein said.

A certain boy from *chutz l'Aretz* had been stricken with a very serious illness. Things had gotten so bad that the boy had lost consciousness, and the doctors had despaired of all hope for his recovery. The boy's parents had given a lot of *tzedakah*, and had split the Heavens with their prayers for their son's recovery. Indeed, the boy's situation had, with Hashem's help, improved! Miraculously, he regained consciousness, but his legs remained in severe danger. The doctors did not think he would ever be able to walk again.

Rav Shteinman was familiar with the situation; he had even sent a letter of encouragement to the boy. "*Nu?*" he asked Rav Zilberstein. "What is the question you had?"

Rav Zilberstein explained, "This young man is traveling to *chutz l'Aretz*, and he is going to be meeting the sick boy. We want to know what he should say to the boy, how he should encourage him."

Rav Shteinman sank into deep thought for a few moments. Then he got up and took a siddur down from the bookshelf. Turning to the young man in the room, he asked, "Do you know the Thirteen *Ikarim* (Principles of Faith) by heart?"

"No," the young man replied sheepishly. "I don't remember all of them by heart."

The room was silent for a moment. Then Rav Shteinman cried out, "*Oy!* Such a shame! Such a shame that you don't know these lines by heart. By these lines I live my whole life!"

He closed his eyes, and hot tears rolled down his cheeks. In a voice trembling with emotion, he said, "With these Thirteen *Ikarim,* the Jews were able to get through concentration camps! With these Thirteen *Ikarim*, the Jews got through Pharaoh, Nevuchadnetzar, and Haman Harasha! All of the *tzaros*, all of the suffering."

Then Rav Shteinman opened his eyes. "Give the boy the greatest *chizuk* possible. Tell him that every day he should say the Thirteen *Ikarim*; that he should think about them; that he should strengthen himself with them! Explain to him that Hakadosh Baruch Hu created everything, He is the One in charge, and the more he strengthens himself with this fact, the healthier he will become! And with Hashem's help," he concluded warmly, "I will send the boy a *brachah* on his wedding day!"

THE PLANE THAT WAS SAVED

Rav Rosengarten, one of Rav Shteinman's closest and most devoted *talmidim*, was leaving the Rosh Yeshivah's house after a visit with him, when a strange thing happened.

Usually, when a guest would leave Rav Shteinman's house, the Rosh Yeshivah would get up and escort him for four *amos* in the house, to fulfill the mitzvah of escorting a guest. Rav Rosengarten was used to this practice of Rav Shteinman's, and expected nothing different on this occasion. But today, when Rav Rosengarten was getting ready to leave, Rav Shteinman rose and began walking with him all the way to the entrance of his house.

Rav Rosengarten felt very uncomfortable. "There's no need for the Rav to exert himself like this," he protested, but the Rosh Yeshivah continued walking with him.

"Really, it's not necessary..." Rav Rosengarten tried again. "The Rav shouldn't..."

But it was to no avail. Rav Shteinman insisted on escorting Rav Rosengarten all the way to the entrance of the house, and then he continued walking with him for a full four *amos* outside of his home, too!

Rav Shteinman's family was very surprised. No one could understand why the Rosh Yeshivah had veered from his normal practice. Why had he escorted Rav Rosengarten so much of the way? But when they tried asking him about it, Rav Shteinman replied simply, "The Rambam brings down that there's a *shemirah* (special protection) to do this."

As can be imagined, this response did little to satisfy everyone's curiosity. If escorting a guest until four *amos* out of the house is indeed a *shemirah*, why didn't Rav Shteinman always follow this practice? But no one questioned the Rosh Yeshivah further about it.

All too soon, it became apparent as to which special *shemirah* Rav Rosengarten needed at this time...

Soon after leaving Rav Shteinman's home, Rav Rosengarten left for the airport, as he had a plane to America to catch. Rav Rosengarten wasn't the only *frum* person on the flight; more than one hundred other *frum* people were traveling with him. Nothing could have prepared any of them for the danger they found themselves in, as the plane on which they were traveling suddenly developed problems with its landing gear, and before long, was headed in the direction of a crash!

Reports of the dangerous situation on board reached the ears of those on land, and worry filled the hearts of the entire Jewish community. Messengers were quickly sent to the homes of the *gedolei hador*, to beg the *gedolim* to *daven* for a *yeshuah* for Rav Rosengarten and the others on that plane.

A few terribly tense hours passed, and then the miracle occurred: the issues with the landing gear were resolved, and the plane landed peacefully on the ground.

Everyone breathed a huge sigh of relief.

Now Rav Shteinman's family understood why he had wanted to escort Rav Rosengarten that extra amount. But when someone made a comment about this to Rav Shteinman himself, he humbly responded, "Even if it helped, it's not because of me—it's because of what the Rambam brings down..."

OBLIGATED TO GIVE A SHIUR

Rav Shteinman's carefulness to keep his word characterized his entire manner of speech. Always when he spoke about something he would do in the future, or about a *shiur* that he was going to give over, he added the word "perhaps" or "possibly," in order to stress from the outset that he was not obligating himself to do it. Rather, he would try his best, and if he didn't end up doing it, it wouldn't be considered as if he didn't keep his word.

It was Erev Rosh Chodesh Elul, in the year 5771, and Rav Shteinman arrived at his yeshivah, Yeshivas Orchos Torah, to *daven* Maariv. He had just returned from a long trip and was feeling exhausted and weak. Right before *davening* began, he made an announcement: "Because I'm a '*ba min haderech* (just coming home from a trip),' I'm really *patur* (exempt) from *davening*, and certainly I'm *patur* from giving the *shiur* that I wanted to say. I'm going to give the *shiur* at a different time instead."

Of course everyone understood, and Maariv began soon after, Rav Shteinman *davening* along with the rest of the yeshivah.

After *davening*, however, there was a surprising change in the plans: The Rosh Yeshivah whispered that he wanted to give the *shiur*! Although unsure as to the reason for the change, everyone in the yeshivah sat down expectantly in their places to hear the *shiur*.

Rav Shteinman was visibly very weak, and it was clear that he was straining himself just to get a few sentences out of his mouth.

"Let me get the speaker system," one of the Rosh Yeshivah's attendants offered. He ran to bring the heavy pieces of equipment that they used for all of Rav Shteinman's *shiurim*, but this time the Rosh Yeshivah didn't wait for him to bring it. He quickly said over a short *shiur* as best as he could, and that was the end of that.

Only afterward did the full picture emerge: Rav Shteinman had thought that the words he'd used while explaining to the people how weak he was—"I'm going to give the *shiur* at a different time instead"—actually *obligated* him to give the *shiur* at a different time. And if he pushed off giving the *shiur* for the next week, or for the next day, or even for another hour—well, who could guarantee that he'd be able to give the *shiur* then? Who could guarantee that there would be "a different time"?

That being the case, Rav Shteinman felt he needed to exert himself to fulfill his obligation right away, no matter what it took. That was why, despite his exhaustion, and despite the fact that the speaker system hadn't even been brought in yet, he quickly delivered the *shiur*.

HASHEM WILL HELP!

Reb Yehoshua Langfeld was a dedicated *ben Torah* who was sitting and learning in *kollel* for already quite a few years. But lately, he was having a tough time making ends meet. His *kollel* was behind on payments, and his wife could not find a good job to help support the family.

Maybe it's time for me to leave kollel *and start working,* Reb Yehoshua began to wonder. *Or, at the very least, maybe I should find a different* kollel*, one that pays on time. But the learning is going so well where I am now! I have such wonderful* chavrusos*, and I'm seeing so much* hatzlachah *in my learning…should I leave all of that, just so I could have an easier time paying the bills?*

Feeling torn, Reb Yehoshua went to speak things over with Rav Shteinman.

As he entered the Rosh Yeshivah's home, his eyes took in the extreme simplicity and poverty of the apartment—the bare walls, the lack of furnishings, the old table and chairs… The question he was going to ask began to lose some of its steam. After all, the Rosh Yeshivah himself was living on so little…how could he, Reb Yehoshua, complain about not having enough money?!

He presented his situation to Rav Shteinman, and the Rosh Yeshivah listened carefully. Then he asked Reb Yehoshua, "Tell me, are you really living in poverty?"

Reb Yehoshua didn't know what to say. After seeing Rav Shteinman's apartment, he was no longer sure what "poverty" meant!

"Do you have bread in the house?" the Rosh Yeshivah prodded.

Reb Yehoshua nodded. Yes, they had bread to eat.

"How about butter?"

Again, Reb Yehoshua nodded. They had butter, too.

"Do you have potatoes?" Rav Shteinman continued.

"Yes, we also have potatoes," Reb Yehoshua said.

"Okay," Rav Shteinman said, smiling at the *avreich*. "You can stay in learning. As for the bills—Hashem will help."

Reb Yehoshua left the Rosh Yeshivah's home, his question answered. Amazingly enough, just a few minutes later, his wife received a call about a certain job she'd been trying to obtain for a long time. The position had suddenly become available! And two days after that, Reb Yehoshua received a check from his *kollel*, for many months' worth of the payment he was owed.

It was just as Rav Shteinman had told him: *Hashem will help.*

AS A ZECHUS FOR THEIR NESHAMOS

av Shteinman was very stringent when it came to matters of *bein adam l'chaveiro* (between man and his fellow). He regularly said over the well-known statement from the Chazon Ish, that the purpose of a person in This World is to go through his entire life without hurting anyone.

"Sometimes a person has grievances toward Hakadosh Baruch Hu," Rav Shteinman once said. "He thinks he is righteous, and that whatever *tzaros* he's going through are for no reason, *chas v'shalom.* It is certainly a terrible mistake for anyone to think or feel this way, but at least no one other than the person himself suffers from this wrong way of thinking. But when a person thinks he is right where there's another person involved—then *everyone* suffers from it."

The following anecdote illustrates just how careful Rav Shteinman was with his *bein adam l'chaveiro*…

One of his students noticed that every morning Rav Shteinman would put a coin into *tzedakah*. It seemed to the student as if there were something special behind this practice, and he wondered about it. One day he finally mustered up the courage to ask the Rosh Yeshivah about the reasoning behind his daily "custom."

The response he received left him speechless.

"Once, many years ago," Rav Shteinman told him, "I had an argument with a certain person. It wasn't *chalilah* a fight, and I was very careful not to hurt him at all—but regardless, I wanted to work on my *middos* and do something good for this person. So ever since this incident years back, I give a coin to *tzedakah* every morning in the person's *zechus*. And I do the same thing for another individual with whom I also once had an argument."

The student just stared in disbelief, feeling tears spring to his eyes, as the Rosh Yeshivah concluded, "Both of these people are no longer alive—they passed away quite a few years ago. But every day I try to 'compensate' the two of them for what happened between us, by doing something good as a *zechus* for their *neshamos*. Even though I didn't hurt them, and they didn't hurt me, you never know—perhaps I *was* a bit guilty for what happened in these situations…"

WHY WAS RAV SHTEINMAN SO FRIGHTENED?

Several *roshei yeshivah* and *talmidei chachamim* were gathered in Rav Shteinman's home for a meeting. They had come to discuss certain public issues with him and to hear his ruling on them.

Suddenly, thunderous noise could be heard coming from the direction of the front door! Everyone in the room turned toward the source of the noise, wondering what was going on.

It soon became clear that the noise was actually the sound of people arguing loudly among themselves just outside the house. As it turned out, there were several young men who felt that they, too, had what to say about the issues being discussed with Rav Shteinman, and they wished to enter the house—if not by invitation, then by force—and join the group so that they could express their burning opinions.

A family member was trying to send these people away, to prevent them from entering the house, but the rabble-rousers outside were having none of that.

The atmosphere in Rav Shteinman's home became tense. The people were worried that an actual riot might break out at any moment. But the expression on the Rosh Yeshivah's face was completely different from everyone else's—it was one of real fear!

A few of the young men outside succeeded in making their way into Rav Shteinman's home. His face pale, Rav Shteinman turned to them, and in a soft voice he asked, "Why are you doing this? Precious *avreichim* like you… Why would you behave in such a rough manner?"

Thankfully, the unpleasant scene ended before long. The young men eventually left, and the meeting participants continued their discussion with the Rosh Yeshivah as before. But the expression of fear that Rav Shteinman had worn during the disruption still filled the minds of those who had seen it. *Why was the Rosh Yeshivah so frightened?* they wondered.

A few days passed, and then a *talmid* dared to ask Rav Shteinman the question that all of them had. "Why was the Rosh Yeshivah so frightened when those rabble-rousers wanted to force their way into the meeting?"

The *talmid* was not expecting the answer that he received.

"When I realized that the people who wanted to enter the house were those who enjoy screaming and protesting," Rav Shteinman said, "I became very afraid that, in my displeasure, I wouldn't react properly, the way I should react. I was petrified that I would *chas v'shalom* offend these people more than the Torah permits…"

A WARM HEART

The Rosh Yeshivah's sensitivity toward other people sometimes reached the point where his actual health could be compromised because of it!

The following story, which took place one summer when Rav Shteinman was giving *shiurim* in Yeshivas Ponovezh, was related by the Rebbetzin *a"h*:

It was very hot outside. Whenever the Rosh Yeshivah arrived at the yeshivah to give his *shiur*, the boys would run to turn on the air conditioner or fan for him, directing the air flow toward his direction so that the cool air would blow straight at him and offer some relief from the intense heat.

Now, Rav Shteinman was naturally a very weak and frail person, and this "favor" that the *bachurim* would do for him was not really a favor at all. Rav Shteinman had no pleasure from the cool air blowing on him; to the contrary, the cold air was actually freezing for him!

"What the Rosh Yeshivah could have easily done," the Rebbetzin would say when telling over this story, "was tell the boys this, and ask them to please *not* direct the cold air of the air conditioner or fan toward him. But the Rosh Yeshivah's sensitivity to the feelings of these young *bachurim*, who, after all, thought they were honoring him, would not allow him to do this. And so he chose instead to suffer in silence from the freezing cold air.

"Because of this," the Rebbetzin would finish off, "whenever I myself would meet up with one of the *bachurim* in the yeshivah, I would beg him to please have pity on my husband's health and to remember to not direct the air conditioner or fan toward him!"

***

When he was already older, Rav Shteinman himself once told his grandson about something similar that he would do:

"In recent years," he related, "there's a *minyan* that comes to my house for *davening* on Shabbos. I never turn on the air conditioner in the house for myself—I'm always afraid I'll be cold and get sick, *chas v'shalom*. But when the people who *daven* here asked to turn it on, I had an idea: I'll let them have the air conditioner on, and I'll just wear an extra, warm layer of clothing. True, this was during the months of Tammuz and Av...but here was a way to let these people have the air conditioner on, as they wanted!"

And that is exactly what Rav Shteinman did.

SOAKED IN COLD WATER

ometimes Rav Shteinman received visitors in his bedroom. One day, a group of his students came into his room to discuss an important issue with him.

There was a *netilas yadayim* basin on the floor, with a full cup of water in it. Due to the lack of space in the room, one of the *talmidim* who had come in picked up the basin and moved it to the pillow on the bed. Then he sat down in his seat and turned his attention to the conversation going on around him.

A few moments later, it happened: the cup of cold water spilled all over the bed—exactly in the place where Rav Shteinman was sitting!

Had this incident happened to anyone else, the person would have jumped up from his place in alarm and dismay—or, at the very least, he would have turned his head, said something about what just happened, moved away a bit...*something*! But the Rosh Yeshivah didn't do anything at all. He simply continued sitting in his place, as if nothing at all had occurred! He didn't turn his head; he didn't even utter a cry. He just went on serenely conversing with his visitors, while his clothing became more and more drenched.

Only after the visitors had finally left the room, and Rav Shteinman was sure that his reaction wouldn't cause pain or embarrassment to the man who had left the water in such an impractical spot, did he quickly get up from his place.

His family was shocked when they grasped what had happened. The water from the *netilas yadayim* cup had gotten everywhere. The Rosh Yeshivah's clothes were sopping wet, the sheets and blanket were soaked, and even the mattress was sodden.

"How was the Rosh Yeshivah able to sit still in his place like that—to the extent that even those around him didn't realize that a cup of cold water had just spilled all over him?!" his family asked in amazement.

Rav Shteinman calmly responded, "Would it have been better for a Yid to become embarrassed? Don't our Sages tell us that a person should throw himself into a fire, rather than have his friend shamed in public?"

***

The following story is another illustration of Rav Shteinman's great sensitivity for the feelings of others:

It was Purim. Rav Shteinman was sitting in his room with a group of *avreichim*, when all of a sudden, a *bachur* who was drunk burst into the room. He began to give a *drashah* in which he praised the Rosh Yeshivah over and over again.

Rav Shteinman, who deeply disliked any type of praise about himself, felt very uncomfortable and turned his head toward the wall. Those present with him in the room saw this and, realizing how unpleasant the scene was for the Rosh Yeshivah, they quickly chased the *bachur* back outside.

For a few long minutes afterward, Rav Shteinman could not be calm. He kept worrying about the incident, and asked again and again whether or not the *bachur* had been offended; if he had been chased away by force; and if they had dealt with him as respectfully as possible...

WITH A WARM HEART

FROM "SHTEINMAN" TO "BERKOWITZ"

A certain *tzedakah* organization, run by a group of dedicated *avreichim*, was seeing much *hatzlachah*, when one day, they received a letter from a different *tzedakah* organization, asking them to please change their name.

"The name of your organization is too similar to ours," the second *tzedakah* organization claimed. "And we were around first. In fact, we feel that the reason you are having such *hatzlachah* is probably because people are confusing you with us!"

Well, the heads of the *tzedakah* organization that received the letter were in no rush to go and change their name, just because the other organization wanted them to do that. Still, just to be sure they were doing the right thing, they decided to check with the *gedolim* about it.

They went to one great *posek* and explained the situation to him. The *posek* thought about the question, and then ruled that the names were not similar enough that the first organization would have to change its name.

"However," the *posek* added, "I think you should go to Rav Shteinman with the question and hear his opinion, too."

Another *posek* told them the exact same thing: he felt that they did not have to change their name, but that Rav Shteinman should be consulted about it, as well.

Now, Rav Shteinman was very familiar with the organization and with the *avreichim* who headed it, and the *avreichim* were confident that, when they would tell the whole story to the Rosh Yeshivah, he would be in agreement with the ruling issued by both *poskim* and would add his own approval to it, too.

But to their great surprise, when Rav Shteinman heard them out, he responded with a sharp question: "Why do you care so much about changing your name a bit, if it will help prevent a *machlokes*? You'll see—nothing bad will come from it!"

The *avreichim* recoiled. They certainly hadn't been expecting a response like that! One of them had the guts to ask, "What if someone would come to the Rosh Yeshivah and ask him to change his name to Berkowitz or Shitrit—would the Rosh Yeshivah agree to do that?"

Rav Shteinman's reply was swift and full of feeling. "Believe me," he said, "that if it were clear to me that this was what the person wanted, and he really felt that if I changed my name it would help him, and by my doing so it would prevent a *machlokes*—then yes, I would change my name to Berkowitz or Shitrit!"

THE BEST SEGULAH OF ALL

When it came to *segulos*, Rav Shteinman's opinion was well known: Many people search high and low for all sorts of different *segulos*, in order to merit a *yeshuah*—and they don't realize that the best *segulah* that exists is simply having the *middah* of *vatranus*—giving in.

"Breaking one's negative *middos*," the Rosh Yeshivah repeatedly said, "is a tried-and-true *segulah*. We find that Sarah Imeinu, who was childless for many years, had Hagar enter her home, in order to work on her *middos*—and Sarah was *zoche* to have Yitzchak. And Rochel Imeinu did the same thing, and she was *zoche* to children, too."

Many times, when people turned to Rav Shteinman in desperate situations, whether they longed to be blessed with children or a *shidduch*, or they had *parnassah* or health problems for which they needed a *yeshuah*, the Rosh Yeshivah told them: "Give in! Just give in! There's no better way to merit a *yeshuah* than being *mevater*!"

Indeed, the following story shows how powerful the *middah* of *vatranus* is:

A bitter fight once broke out between the head of a certain *chessed* organization and one of his senior managers. It reached a point where the head of the organization felt he could no longer tolerate having the manager employed by him, and he decided to fire him and hire someone else to fill the position. But before taking that drastic measure, he decided to speak it over with Rav Shteinman. He told him the whole story, about how his relationship with this manager had soured, and he asked if he had the right to fire him.

Rav Shteinman stroked his beard while thinking about the question. For a full few minutes, there was complete silence in the room. Finally, Rav Shteinman spoke.

"It's true that halachically, you would be allowed to fire him. If your relationship with your manager is not good, you're not obligated to continue employing him.

"But," the Rosh Yeshivah's voice rose, "aren't you and your wife waiting to have children, already for many long years? Look—a rare opportunity has just been presented to you! If you can be *mevater*, overlook the whole fight, and keep this manager employed, you will be gaining an unbelievable *zechus*. And that *zechus* may be the one you need to merit having a child! So be strong—and give in!"

Tears filled the man's eyes, and a sob caught in his throat as he nodded his agreement to the Rosh Yeshivah's words. "Okay," he whispered. "I'm going to be *mevater*..."

A year later, the whole city of Bnei Brak cried along with the man, this time tears of joy, as Rav Shteinman was the *sandek* at the *bris* of his baby boy.

WITH A WARM HEART

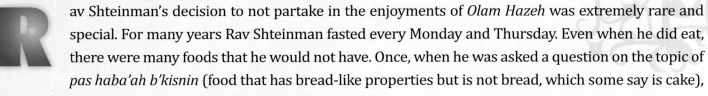

THE UNEATEN YOGURT

Rav Shteinman's decision to not partake in the enjoyments of *Olam Hazeh* was extremely rare and special. For many years Rav Shteinman fasted every Monday and Thursday. Even when he did eat, there were many foods that he would not have. Once, when he was asked a question on the topic of *pas haba'ah b'kisnin* (food that has bread-like properties but is not bread, which some say is cake), he remarked, "I don't understand all the hype about this. I haven't tasted cake since I was ten years old…"

Obviously, these types of behaviors are not for every person or every situation. It can only work for the kind of person whose every strength, and whose entire body and soul, are submerged in the study of Torah and working on one's *middos*.

The following story testifies to the greatness of Rav Shteinman in this area.

The Rosh Yeshivah had just been in the hospital, where he had received strong antibiotics for an infection. He had returned home, but was in very weak condition; the antibiotics had really knocked him out. According to the doctors' recommendations, if he would eat foods containing live, "good" bacteria, such as yogurt, it would help his body regain its strength.

Rav Shteinman's family surrounded his bed. Anxious for his health, his children tried to convince him to follow the doctors' advice and eat yogurt. "Abba, it's a matter of health! Please eat it!" they begged him.

But Rav Shteinman, who had never put yogurt into his mouth before, did not want to taste this food now, in his old age. "All my life I held myself back from eating delicacies. Now I should break my custom?" he asked.

His children did not let up. They begged and they pleaded, until Rav Shteinman was unable to refuse them anymore, and, due to his extreme weakness, he agreed to eat some yogurt.

Smiles of relief broke out on his children's faces, and a *talmid* quickly ran to get some yogurt with the best *hechsher*. The container of yogurt was brought to Rav Shteinman, along with a spoon. The Rosh Yeshivah used all of his strength to sit up in bed, and he dished out a bit of the yogurt on the spoon. Then he looked at the spoon of yogurt in his hand, closed his eyes, and was about to make a *Shehakol*…when suddenly, as if a fighting spirit had been ignited in him, he put down the spoon and pushed the container of yogurt away.

"No, no!" he cried. "Something that I never ate for my entire life—I cannot eat it now, in my old age!" He turned to his children. "Forgive me for having troubled you to get it," he said, "but please understand my heart…"

WHEN SHOULD ONE NOT BE STRINGENT?

Even those who were close to Rav Shteinman knew little of all the many *chumros* (stringencies) and practices that he accepted upon himself. He was extremely careful to hide his *chumros* from other people.

Once, a grandson turned to him with a question: "I recently saw a picture of Zeide drinking wine. But doesn't Zeide have a custom, already for many years, not to eat meat or drink wine during the week? Why did Zeide break that custom and drink wine on a weekday?"

Rav Shteinman responded, "You should know, my precious grandson, that although I am *makpid* not to drink wine during the week, when people serve me wine in public, I don't refrain from drinking it. The reason for this is because I don't want to publicize my *chumros*, and also I don't want to hurt my hosts' feelings…"

(Obviously, he would only take this approach with *chumros* of his own—not with *chumros* that pertained to actual halachah.)

***

The following story is another example of how Rav Shteinman balanced his many *chumros* and personal customs with his exceptional *bein adam l'chaveiro*:

It was the year the Rebbetzin passed away. Pesach was approaching, the first one without the Rebbetzin at Rav Shteinman's side. The Rosh Yeshivah approached his attendants on Erev Yom Tov and asked if they could prepare water in advance for him for the whole Pesach. (This is a certain *chumra* that is practiced by some for Pesach.)

His attendants wondered: *Mah nishtanah*? The Rosh Yeshivah had never had this *chumra* before. Why was this year different from the other years with regard to this stringency?

Rav Shteinman's response to their question left them moved beyond words.

"As long as the Rebbetzin was alive," he said, tears in his eyes, "there was no room for this *chumra*, as to keep it would have been hard on her. But now that, unfortunately, the Rebbetzin is no longer with us, there is no reason not to try keeping the *chumra*…

"It's praiseworthy and it's good to have *chumros*," the Rosh Yeshivah stated in conclusion. "But it can never be on someone else's account!"

This was also the reason why Rav Shteinman refrained from giving his *haskamah* to a *sefer* which discussed the *chumra* of not drinking water that was left uncovered—even though he himself was very strict about keeping this *chumra*. He was afraid that some *bnei Torah* would try to keep this stringency at the expense of their *shalom bayis*—and Rav Shteinman would never agree to being *makpid* about something at the expense of another person.

KIBUD AV V'EIM

Rav Shteinman's presence at Torah gatherings offered much *chizuk* to all those who attended them. In fact, many people participated in these gatherings just to hear his words.

Because of this, Rav Shteinman was usually very willing to come and speak at Torah gatherings. But once, when a *rav* approached him with a request to speak at a *yom iyun* on the topic of *kibud av v'eim*, the Rosh Yeshivah shook his head.

"I'm sorry," he said, "but I can't."

The *rav* tried to convince Rav Shteinman to change his mind. He explained how much *chizuk* the participants would receive from seeing Rav Shteinman there and hearing him speak. But the Rosh Yeshivah stood firm in his refusal.

"But why?" the *rav* finally asked.

Rav Shteinman explained. "Many years ago, when I was a boy of ten, my mother *a"h* asked me to eat a certain food. I didn't find that food appealing, and I refused to eat it. I didn't fulfill my mother's request. I'm afraid," he said, the pain evident in his voice, "that I can't speak to others on the topic of *kibud av v'eim*, if I myself am so imperfect in this area…"

The *rav* was astounded. Such was the level of sensitivity that Rav Shteinman had toward the mitzvah of *kibud av v'eim*!

It was only after much effort and persuasion on the *rav's* part that Rav Shteinman agreed to speak at the gathering, even in his "imperfect state."

The Rebbetzin *a"h*, too, was outstanding in the mitzvah of *kibud av v'eim*. During World War II, when the Nazis *yemach shemam* reached Antwerp, where the Rebbetzin's family lived, the family fled to France. But the Nazis eventually caught up with them there, and they arrested Rav Shammai Shraga, the Rebbetzin's father. They wanted to kill him, but the family was able to bribe them with money and Rav Shammai Shraga was set free.

This happened three times. But when the Nazis arrested Rav Shammai Shraga for the fourth time, the family was not able to bribe them. The Nazis took Rav Shammai Shraga out to kill him…and just then, the Rebbetzin jumped in front of her father.

"Shoot me!" she cried. "Kill me! Just leave my father alone…"

The accursed Nazis didn't pay attention to her cries, and they killed Rav Shammai Shraga. But the *mesirus nefesh* and *kibud av v'eim* that the Rebbetzin displayed will be remembered for generations and generations.

HUMILIATION? WHAT A WONDERFUL GIFT!

av Shteinman frequently related the praises of those who accept humiliation with love, often quoting from the *Peirush Hamishnah la'Rambam* about how a certain chassid felt true joy at the time that someone was embarrassing and belittling him in public. Sometimes, when Rav Shteinman spoke on this subject, he became emotional, and his eyes filled with tears.

The Rosh Yeshivah was someone who practiced what he preached, as the following story will show…

It was during a public gathering in which many important people were participating. A certain frivolous and *chutzpahdik* individual tried to approach the Rosh Yeshivah and make fun of him. Before the other participants were able to get him away from there, he managed to call Rav Shteinman quite a few shameful names.

Did the incident cause Rav Shteinman pain? Not at all! To the contrary, he actually derived much *enjoyment* from it! The next day, after his weekly *shiur* in the Ponovezh *kollel*, he turned to one of the prominent *avreichim* with whom he was close, and, with a big smile on his face, he said, "Ah…you didn't merit to have it…" It was clear that the Rosh Yeshivah was referring to the humiliation that he'd received the day before. "You didn't merit to have it, but I did!"

***

A different time, when Rav Shteinman gave over his opinion—*daas Torah*—about a certain issue pertaining to the *Chareidi* public, a few people who opposed what he was saying decided that they knew better than him. They actually got up and began to publicly protest against him. One of them even had the terrible chutzpah to scribble insulting words on Rav Shteinman's door.

The next day, a *talmid* of the Rosh Yeshivah saw what the person had done. Horrified, he ran to get a knife so he could scrape away the writing from the door.

Later, Rav Shteinman heard about what his *talmid* had done, and he became very upset. He called over the *talmid* and, in a pained voice, asked him, "Why? Why did you do this? Don't I need the humiliation?"

The *talmid* was frightened. "The Rav should forgive me…I only meant well…" he stammered.

Rav Shteinman sighed. "I don't hold anything against you—I know that you only meant well. But you should know, I lost out because of this." Then he explained. "Surely you remember that in America, they gave me too much honor. I need the humiliation now, in order that the honor I was given should not take away from my *Olam Haba*…"

DO YOU PREFER HONOR— OR OLAM HABA?

I t's important to realize," Rav Shteinman often said over, "that any honor given to a person takes away from his *Olam Haba*! One should run far, far away from honor!"

This tendency of Rav Shteinman's, to run far away from honor, was already apparent back when he was young, as can be seen from the following story...

Many years ago, at the time when Rav Shteinman was a *rosh yeshivah* in Kfar Saba, he once paid a visit to the Chazon Ish. The Chazon Ish treated him with much honor, and when Rav Shteinman left, he escorted him all the way to the gate of his house, which was what the Chazon Ish did whenever he had great and important visitors.

All those who were present were astounded at the scene of the Chazon Ish giving this degree of honor to such a young *rosh yeshivah*, but Rav Shteinman himself seemed to actually be suffering from this treatment. He returned to his home in Kfar Saba, went to his room, and burst into bitter sobs. For a full hour, he cried over his *Olam Haba*, which he was sure had become lessened due to the great honor that the Chazon Ish had given him.

Later on in his life, too, when his name had already become well known to the world, whenever Rav Shteinman visited *chutz l'Aretz* in order to spread Torah, and people gave him tremendous honor there—he would close himself up in his room and cry and cry about it.

Rav Shteinman reacted this way not only when he himself was being honored, but also when others were. Many times, when a wealthy individual came to him, and people introduced the person to him by way of extreme praise ("This man supports so many *yeshivos*...he's *mamash* from the biggest *baalei tzedakah* in the world..."), Rav Shteinman looked pityingly at the person whose *sechar* in *Olam Haba* may have been lessened due to the honor he was receiving, and he hinted to the one who was praising him to please stop harming the wealthy man...

As the Rosh Yeshivah explained it, "What a shame it would be, for the man to lose out on some of his reward in *Olam Haba*, just because people give him praise in This World! Is it worth it for him to receive his reward here, in *Olam Hazeh*, in the form of honor?!"

SOFT—AND ALSO STRICT

av Shteinman was known to be an extremely soft and gentle person. However, if something related to a *hashkafah* issue, he became very strict; he would only tolerate the correct course. In situations like these, the Rosh Yeshivah's pure mind—his true *daas Torah*—became readily apparent.

There was a certain man with whom Rav Shteinman was close. Beyond their personal acquaintance of many years, the Rosh Yeshivah felt deep *hakaras hatov* to this man's family, who helped him tremendously when he first came to Eretz Yisrael many years ago. Whenever this person would come into Rav Shteinman's home, the Rosh Yeshivah's face would light up, and he would show him much love and warmth.

This man had a job that involved helping out the *Chareidi avreichim* who were drafted into the army. He was to make sure they were able to maintain their high standards even within the army's framework. However, at a certain point, the man's responsibilities broadened to include actively encouraging *avreichim* to enlist, by promoting the favorable conditions the army promised them.

When Rav Shteinman heard about this, he was horrified. Could it be? Could someone actually have the chutzpah to encourage *avreichim* to leave the *beis midrash* and enlist in the army?!

The next time the man came to the Rosh Yeshivah's home for a *brachah*, Rav Shteinman did not receive him warmly like usual. To the contrary, he made it very clear how upset he was. Even before the man could open his mouth, Rav Shteinman raised his refined voice and, with obvious pain, he rebuked him: "*Oy!* Are you the one who is actually causing the *avreichim* to leave their holy Torah learning?" he asked, with tears in his eyes.

"Don't touch my anointed one!" he quoted, adding, "If someone closes his Gemara because of you, you will have committed a very grave sin!"

Yes, Rav Shteinman's softness and refined nature were well known. But when there was a need for it, the Rosh Yeshivah could be the strongest of the strong, and he showed no favoritism, even to those close to him.

Another time, a high school principal who had decided not to accept certain girls into his school, for reasons that were not right, came to see Rav Shteinman. The Rosh Yeshivah had heard about this principal's decision, and he saw it as a serious wrongdoing on his part. But the principal was sure that, due to his close relationship with him, the Rosh Yeshivah would not rebuke him for this.

How wrong he was! Soon after he entered the Shteinman home, the Rosh Yeshivah turned to him with extremely harsh *mussar*: "*Oy!* Don't you know that one day you will stand in judgment before Hashem? There is judgment, and there is a Judge! How are you not afraid of the *Yom Hadin*?!"

WHO ARE THE TRULY LUCKY ONES?

The following story happened in the winter of the year 5763. The financial situation of the *kollel yungeleit* was very hard at the time, to the point where many of them barely had any food to eat. These dedicated young men fought with all their strength not to close their Gemaras and go out to work.

Rav Shteinman felt the pain of these *yungeleit*, and he did whatever he could to help them get through this tough *nisayon*.

One day, a wealthy and respected individual came to see Rav Shteinman. He had flown in from *chutz l'Aretz* specifically to do his part in helping out the *kollel avreichim*, and, knowing that Rav Shteinman was the top authority when it came to the world of *Litvishe avreichim*, he made his way to the Rosh Yeshivah's home. As it turned out, however, despite this man's good intentions, what he had in mind to do for the *yungeleit* was quite contrary to what the Torah world really needed…

The rich man entered the Rosh Yeshivah's room, sat down, and began outlining his plan: "I thought of a wonderful way to help out the *kollel avreichim*. I want to fund a training program for them. Like this, they'll have a much easier time finding a job, and they'll be able to provide for their families in an honorable way!" As he spoke, he withdrew a check from his wallet…made out for *$10,000,000*! "*Kavod harav*," the man said emotionally, "this is my humble donation toward making my plan a reality!"

He expected Rav Shteinman's face to light up at this offer. Surely the Rosh Yeshivah would embrace and bless him for his extraordinary donation!

But not a muscle twitched in Rav Shteinman's face. He looked at the check and then at the rich man, and, in a voice filled with pain, he said, "The *olam haTorah* needs to be strengthened, not weakened! We need to *increase* Torah learning, not to decrease it! It is forbidden to touch the *olam haTorah*! It is absolutely forbidden!"

The rich man was shocked. Before his disbelieving eyes, the Rosh Yeshivah gently pushed the check back toward him and said, "If it's the poverty of *bnei Torah* that is worrying you, you should realize that being poor has many advantages over being rich. Throughout all of *galus*, it was specifically the poor people who held their ground and remained Torah Jews no matter what.

"And as an aside," the Rosh Yeshivah added, "if you think that the poverty-stricken *avreichim* are an unfortunate lot, go and ask them about it. They themselves will tell you that there's no one in the whole world who is luckier than they are!"

Speechless, the rich man returned the check to his wallet. The lesson he'd received in Rav Shteinman's room that day, on the value of Torah learning, was one he would never forget.

WITH A WARM HEART

FROM HIS OWN MONEY

I t was two weeks before Purim. While the rest of the Jewish world busied themselves with *mishloach manos* preparations and finding costumes, the *gabbaim* of the Kupat Ha'ir *tzedakah* organization were busy with their *matanos l'evyonim* collections.

They visited the homes of many *gedolei hador* and received donations from them. What they wanted to do was to publicize the fact that "the *gedolei hador* donated to Kupat Ha'ir, and the *gabbaim* will distribute their money to poor people on Purim!" in order to spur other people to donate to the *tzedakah*, as well.

When the *gabbaim* of Kupat Ha'ir arrived at Rav Shteinman's home, he greeted them warmly. Then he took out a 100-dollar bill from his pocket and gave it to them. But when the *gabbaim* asked him to write and sign on the fact that he'd donated to Kupat Ha'ir, intending to publicize this statement for all to see, Rav Shteinman refused, saying, "I can't sign to a lie."

What lie is the Rosh Yeshivah referring to? the *gabbaim* wondered to themselves, though none of them dared ask the question aloud. They tried to politely ask again if the Rosh Yeshivah could simply sign that he'd donated money, but Rav Shteinman's response was the same. "What can I do?" he said to them. "I can't sign to a lie."

The *gabbaim* didn't try to press the issue further. They understood that obviously the Rosh Yeshivah was aware of something they were not, and so they left the house without his signature.

Two days later, Rav Shteinman asked for one of the *gabbaim* of Kupat Ha'ir to be called back to his home. When the *gabbai* entered his apartment, the Rosh Yeshivah took out some money from his pocket, gave it to the *gabbai*, and said, "Here is money for *matanos l'evyonim*. Now I am able to write and sign that I gave money for Kupat Ha'ir to distribute as *matanos l'evyonim*."

Before the surprised *gabbai* could ask for any explanation, Rav Shteinman explained: "Two days ago, I didn't have any money of my own on me, not even a penny. The 100 dollars that I gave you was not from my personal money—it was from the *tzedakah* account that I take care of.

"*Nu*," he continued, as if speaking to himself, "how can I write that I gave some of my money to *tzedakah*—if the money I gave was not mine?! It would have been a lie! Today, though, I received some money of my own. Now I am able to give it to Kupat Ha'ir *and* to write, with a full heart, that I gave some of my money to *tzedakah*!"

SEFER AYELES HASHACHAR

av Shteinman honored the Rebbetzin to a very great extent. When she became ill and was bedridden, many times the Rosh Yeshivah himself would bring her food, and he would sit by her side and wait until she finished eating.

The name Rav Shteinman gave for his *sefarim* on *Shas*, *Ayeles Hashachar*, actually has a lot to do with the honor and respect with which he treated his Rebbetzin.

When the Rosh Yeshivah was ready to publish his first *sefer* on *Shas*, he decided to do it anonymously. However, since it is brought down from the Roke'ach that a person who writes a *sefer* should hint to his name in the title of the *sefer*, Rav Shteinman decided to have the letters *aleph*, *yud*, and *lamed* somewhere in the title, to hint to his name: Aharon Yehudah Leib.

One day, before any title was decided on, the Rebbetzin came home with an interesting piece of information. She had heard that a certain *rav*, who had recently written a *sefer*, had hinted to both his name *and* his wife's name in the title of the book. Rav Shteinman, who had been thinking at that exact time about a title to use for his *sefer*, heard what the Rebbetzin said—and suddenly his decision was made!

If I hint to the Rebbetzin's name in the name of my sefer, *just like that* rav *did,* he thought, *it will give her such pleasure! That's exactly what I'm going to do.*

And so it was. The Rosh Yeshivah decided to call his series of *sefarim*, *Ayeles Hashachar*: the *aleph*, *yud*, and *lamed* stand for his name, and the *tav* at the end stands for Tamar, the name of the Rebbetzin.

When Rav Shteinman's *talmidim* heard about the name he had chosen for his *sefer*, a few of them mentioned the fact that in *Tehillim*, the *mefarshim* tell us how the word "*ayeles*" does not suggest positive things. But Rav Shteinman did not change his mind about his title.

"The *sefer* will be called *Ayeles Hashachar*, in honor of the Rebbetzin and in order to give her pleasure," he said decisively. And in doing so, he taught his students a great lesson on the subject of a husband showing honor to his wife.

THE CHAPTER THAT WAS TAKEN APART

av Shteinman's genius and greatness in Torah learning was well known ever since he was a child; he was always found poring over his Gemara in the *beis midrash*, with tremendous *hasmadah*. His series of *sefarim* on *Shas*, *Ayeles Hashachar*, is further proof to his extraordinary capabilities when it comes to Torah learning.

Ayeles Hashachar contains numerous thought-out and complex Torah pieces and chapters that the Rosh Yeshivah wrote on the Gemara. Through these brilliant pieces, one can clearly see his greatness in learning... but just as clearly, once can see his humility and his care for the honor of others.

Rav Shteinman was once sitting in his room, going over the volume of *Ayeles Hashachar* on *Maseches Bava Kamma*. The *sefer* had many intricate chapters in it, and everything was just about done; the *sefer* seemed ready for print.

He was just putting in some last-minute comments and revisions, when suddenly, a cloud seemed to pass over his face, and a great sigh escaped his mouth. What had happened? What had he just noticed?

The first chapter in the *sefer* explored the opinion of the Brisker Rav on a certain topic. In this chapter, the Rosh Yeshivah had gathered many proofs, from all over *Bava Kamma*, against the Brisker Rav's opinion. Rav Shteinman had written his *sefer* very carefully. He had taken great pains when writing each word, and he had given the Brisker Rav much honor and respect in the *sefer*. Still, while going over the *sefer* now, Rav Shteinman was not happy with how things were.

Is it proper to begin a sefer *with an entire chapter bringing proofs against the Brisker Rav's opinion?* he thought to himself. Then and there he made up his mind: *No, it's not. I must do something about this.*

Rav Shteinman decided to *take apart the whole chapter* and put all the proofs he had gathered in different places throughout the *sefer*; each proof would go in the section of the *sefer* that discussed the part of the Gemara where the proof was originally found.

And, without any hesitation, that's exactly what he did. He sat for many hours and took apart the entire chapter that he had worked so hard to construct.

True, the original, complete chapter had done a better job highlighting the opinion of the Brisker Rav. True, it wasn't a small thing to take apart an entire chapter like this, especially when the *sefer* was just about ready to go to print. But for Rav Shteinman, it was all worth it—just so there would not be even the tiniest slight to the honor of the Brisker Rav.

WILL HE EVEN NEED THE SURGERY AT ALL?

O ne Friday, a few members of a certain family entered Rav Shteinman's room, looking very anxious and tense. A close relative of theirs was supposed to undergo surgery that Sunday, and the doctors were in disagreement about how the surgery should be done. They had left the decision—which was quite a serious one—up to the family. Not knowing what to do, but having faith in *daas Torah*, the family turned to Rav Shteinman for guidance.

The Rosh Yeshivah sat and listened to the family members in silence. Once he'd heard the specifics from them, he thought for a few moments, and then he began to advise them about how to proceed with the surgery. The family members asked him about some details, and he answered each and every one of their questions.

Finally a clear picture was emerging for the family—an understandable way as to how the surgery should be done. Sighs of relief were heard throughout the room.

Suddenly, without any warning, Rav Shteinman put his head down in his hands. He remained in that position, deep in thought, for some time, his face aflame with holiness. A hush fell over the room as the visitors waited respectfully.

Then Rav Shteinman raised his head and said, "And it's possible that he won't even need the surgery at all!"

Was this a *nevuah*? Was it *ruach hakodesh*? The family didn't have to wait long to find out…

Sunday dawned, the day of the surgery. As the sick man's family gathered in his room, waiting for the hospital staff to begin the preoperative preparations, they were suddenly informed that the doctors had unexpectedly encountered some new medical findings, which seemed to indicate the usage of a different course of treatment for the patient. The doctors were meeting right now to discuss this and would keep the family posted about it.

An hour later, the doctors came into the patient's room with wonderful news: "We don't need to do the surgery, after all! With Hashem's help, the patient can recover from his illness even without having surgery!"

And so it was, just as Rav Shteinman had said!

AHAVAS HATORAH

The study of Torah is equal to all else!" Rav Shteinman would say, again and again, to all those who came to see him.

Once on Rosh Hashanah, the Rosh Yeshivah turned to a *talmid* and said to him, "I am afraid!"

"What is the Rosh Yeshivah afraid of?" the *talmid* asked.

Rav Shteinman answered, "I'm afraid that every morning I'll be asked to be *sandek* at a *bris*, and every evening I'll be invited to a *chasunah*—and then there won't be any time left for me to learn Torah!"

Rav Shteinman's *talmidim* can well attest to the great *ahavas haTorah* that he had. One *talmid* related the following:

"The Rosh Yeshivah sometimes took a nap before giving his *shiur*, to give himself some strength after having toiled in learning for many hours straight. When the Rebbetzin was alive, she would come to wake him up, and I would see an amazing thing happen. Even before he would fully awaken, he would reach for the pages of his *sefer Ayeles Hashachar*! Only once the *sefer* was tightly in his hands would the Rosh Yeshivah open his eyes."

Then there were the many times when visitors came into Rav Shteinman's room while he was immersed in his learning. The Rosh Yeshivah paid no attention whatsoever to the fact that his room was crowded with people. Visitors could have been surrounding him on all sides, there could have been a commotion going on, time could have been passing—but if he was in the middle of a *blatt* Gemara, nothing else but the Gemara existed.

As the Rosh Yeshivah would say, "We must toil lovingly in the Torah always. Always, always…"

THE BLACKENED WALL

T he utter simplicity that screamed from every corner of Rav Shteinman's apartment astounded many of his visitors. Often, the people who came to him, whether to ask him a question or to receive a *brachah*, were influenced by the level of simplicity in his home more than anything else.

Throughout the years, many of Rav Shteinman's *talmidim* and close acquaintances made numerous attempts to have his home renovated, or expanded, or even just re-painted. But Rav Shteinman always said no, gently but firmly.

"*Olam Hazeh* is just a hallway," he said. "We don't busy ourselves too much with a hallway." And he added, "To the degree that we minimize our *Olam Hazeh*, that's how much greater our *Olam Haba* will be!"

There was once a painter who lived near Rav Shteinman's home. The painter loved and admired Rav Shteinman greatly, and begged him, again and again, to let him have the *zechus* of painting his apartment. But the Rosh Yeshivah would not allow it.

"However," the Rosh Yeshivah told the painter, "if you want to paint just the hall at the entrance to the house— that you could do."

When the painter heard this, he became very excited. He ran to get his painting equipment and then immediately got started on the job, painting the hall at the entrance to Rav Shteinman's home with painstaking dedication.

Finally he was finished, and the hall looked fresh and beautiful.

Some time passed. One Friday night, a flame from the oil lamp hanging on the wall in Rav Shteinman's home suddenly burst, causing the wall to become blackened. A family member couldn't resist mentioning that this was the same wall that had just been painted, by the man who had begged and insisted on being allowed to do something for Rav Shteinman's home. Was this some kind of sign from *Shamayim*?

"You should know," the Rosh Yeshivah answered firmly, "that the reason why this incident happened is because we changed our *hanhagah* and allowed the wall to be painted."

ONE LESS QUESTION IN OLAM HABA

It was on Purim. A *talmid* knocked on the door, entered, and handed Rav Shteinman an envelope with 5,000 dollars in it.

"This money is for the *avreich* Reb Ploni," the *talmid* said. "He is embarrassed to take *tzedakah*, although he really could use it. He'll refuse to accept the money—unless the Rav gives it to him."

Rav Shteinman agreed to give the money to the *avreich*, and he hid the envelope in a safe place. But a short time later, when the Rosh Yeshivah went to get the money so he could give it to the *avreich*, he was dismayed to discover that the envelope was gone!

The Rosh Yeshivah was very distressed, and he looked high and low for the missing envelope. His family joined him in the search, and they spent an entire hour looking for it—but to no avail. The money had disappeared, as if the ground had swallowed it up. Apparently, someone had taken advantage of the Purim atmosphere in the house and, finding the money, had stolen it for himself.

A few hours passed, and Rav Shteinman asked for the *talmid* who had originally brought him the envelope to come back to his home. When the *talmid* came in, Rav Shteinman said to him, "According to halachah, I wasn't a *shomer* (watcher) for the money, but rather a *shaliach* (messenger to deliver something)—and therefore I would not be responsible for what happened to the money.

"However," he continued, "soon enough I will be called to the World of Truth, and I'll be asked there how careful I was with regard to this money which I was supposed to give to the *avreich*. Perhaps, *chas v'shalom*, there will be a claim against me for this…"

The *talmid* tried to protest, but the Rosh Yeshivah stopped him. "I am *b'ezras Hashem* going to pay back the money. So far, I already gave the *avreich* a few hundred dollars, which I had on me. And I sent a request to a *gemach* to borrow the rest of the amount. I hope to get the money from the *gemach* soon, and I'll give it all to the *avreich*. And then, as soon as I can, I'll pay up my loan from the *gemach*.

"We need to realize," he said emotionally, "that it's worth it to spend *150,000 dollars*, in order to avoid even one question in *Olam Haba*!"

And so the Rosh Yeshivah took the *gemach* loan upon himself and gave the money to the *avreich*. It took him a complete year until he was able to pay back the whole loan…but for Rav Shteinman, it was all worth it, because now he would be asked one less question in *Olam Haba*.

A LESSON IN CHINUCH

The following story shows how true methods of *chinuch* are found in the Torah and by the *gedolim* who toil in the Torah their whole lives.

The parents of a ten-year-old boy came to speak with Rav Shteinman, looking anxious and upset.

"*Kavod harav*," the father began tearfully, "something terrible is going on in our home! Our son has been caught stealing again and again. He steals from his friends and his parents—money, candies, games… We don't know what to do about it! No matter how many times we've tried to explain to him about the severity of stealing, no matter how many times we've punished him or tried to offer him prizes—nothing has helped! We brought our son to many *chinuch* experts, people who are certified professionals…but none of the strategies or advice that they gave us are working. It's like our son is addicted to stealing, *Rachmana litzlan*!" The father's voice caught on a sob.

Rav Shteinman thought quietly for a few minutes. Then he began to speak. "You should know, my son," he addressed the father, "that once a person stumbles in stealing and he tastes the benefits from it, it's very hard to get him to stop. But in our holy Torah we find the way to do it!"

"And what is that way?" the father asked, his ears perking up.

"Well," Rav Shteinman said, "it says in the Torah that if a person steals an ox and sells it, he must repay the value of the ox five times. In comparison to that, if a person steals a sheep and sells it, he must only repay the value of it four times. Why? Because the person who stole the sheep had to have carried it on his shoulders while he was running with it, and this would have certainly caused him embarrassment. (An ox, which is too heavy to carry, would have been led by the thief instead, which does not involve this embarrassment.) Due to the embarrassment that he suffered, we deduct from the amount that he has to pay back."

The Rosh Yeshivah stroked his beard. "We learn from this," he said, "that *bushah*—embarrassment—is the one emotion that can have an effect on a thief. Because even for this thief, whom no one forced to steal, we take into consideration the embarrassment that he surely suffered when he was carrying the sheep on his shoulders.

"My advice for you," he continued, "is that every time you catch your son stealing, *chalilah*, you take him to the person he stole from and have your son himself return the item to him. The embarrassment he'll suffer from this will have an effect on him, and he will stop stealing."

The boy's parents took Rav Shteinman's advice and immediately began to follow it. The next time they caught their son stealing, they insisted that he go and return the stolen item himself. The boy became hysterical and refused to go, crying, "I can't bring it back to them myself! Then they'll know that I took it!"

Of course the parents did not give the boy a choice, and he was forced to undergo the embarrassment of having people realize that he'd stolen something from them.

As you can imagine, it did not take long for the parents to see results from Rav Shteinman's advice. After just a short while, their son completely stopped stealing.